Managing Budgets and Cash flows

Contents

Chapter 1-Introduction   11

Purpose of Budgeting   11

Forecast of income and expenditure   12

Tool for decision making   12

Monitoring business performance   12

Sample budget spreadsheet   13

Budgeting Principles   13

Be conservative not optimistic   13

Team work and consultation   13

Allow plenty of time   15

Provide Training   16

Get Sign Off   16

Cashflow and Business   17

Important Cash Flow Basics   17

Profit Does Not Equal Good Cash Flow   18

Find Out Your Breakeven Point   18

You Can't Control What You Don't Measure

How To Fix Cash Flow Problem In Your Business – 5 Tips 19

Short-Term Financing   19

Long-Term Financing   19

Speed Up Recovery Of Receivables   19

Liquidate Cash Tied Up With Assets 21

Delay Your Payables 22

Best Practices For Managing A Healthy Cash Flow 22

Identify Business Risks & Prepare In Advance 22

Have a Separate Bank Account For Your Business 23

Always Keep Buffer Money 23

Implement A Better System To Manage Cash Flow 24

Cut Costs, Control Cash Outflows 24

Keep Your Cash Growing 24

Chapter 2-An Introduction to Basic Bookkeeping **29**

Business activities of a company or enterprise 29

What information must be kept?

The advantages of a good bookkeeping system for your 31
business

How to record the information you need 33

Proprietary systems 33

The Cash Book System (single entry. 34

Example 1-The sales account book 36

Example 2-The Purchases Account Book 37

Example 3-Cash Receipt Book 38

Example 4-Cheque/bank transfer Payment Books 39

Example 5-Petty Cash Book 40

Example 6- The General Day Book or Journal   41

Invoices   42

Example Invoice   42

VAT   43

The Double Entry System   43

Computerised Accounting Systems   43

Main points from Chapter 2   47

Chapter 3-Management Accounting-Budgets and   **51**
Cashflows Generally

Management Accounting   51

Control of Cash-flows into and out of a business   52

Budgets   53

Formulating budgets   54

Cash flow considerations   54

Example monthly budgeted Profit and Loss account   56

Main Points from Chapter 3   59

Chapter 4-The Process of Setting Budgets   **61**

Format of the Budget   63

Costs involved in business   63

Fixed and variable costs   63

Semi-variable costs   64

Selling expenses   64

Budgeting sales income   65

Who should carry out the sales forecasting   65

Creating the budget-A Publishing Company   65

Arriving at price-price budgeting   67

Example - Direct and indirect costs   68

Costs of production   71

Break even analysis   71

Calculating the break even point   71

Internal budgeting-budgeting for expected overheads
and capital items   72

Budgeting for overheads   74

Budgeting for capital items   78

Example of an administration budget   80

Example of an overall revenue budget   81

Main points from Chapter 4   82

Chapter 5-Cash Flow Management   **85**

The cash flow forecast   85

Forecasting cash flow   87

Debtors   87

Example cashflow forecast   89

The forecasting of other income   92

Forecasting expenditure   92

Salaries and wages and employers contributions   93

Payments for use of energy   93

Payments for rent/service charge   93

Bank and interest charges on overdrafts, loans   94
and hire purchase

Value Added Tax   94

Accounting for VAT on a cash accounting basis   96

Main points from Chapter 5   97

Chapter 6-Monitoring Budgets and Cashflow   101

Example-Monitoring cashflow   102

Monitoring budgets   104

The use of financial ratios for monitoring budgets and
cash flow   105

profit ratios   106

Efficiency ratios   108

Liquidity ratios   109

The security interval   113

Solvency ratios   113

Main points from chapter 6   116

Chapter 7-Using Technology   **119**

Using a spreadsheet   119

Advantages of spreadsheets   121

Disadvantages of using a spreadsheet   121

Sample Spreadsheet   122

Useful addresses and websites

Glossary of terms

Index

****

1.

OVERVIEW OF THE IMPORTANCE OF BUDGETS AND CASHFLOWS IN THE CONTEXT OF BUSINESS

Chapter 1

Introduction

In this brief book, which is intended for those new to business, and who need basic advice concerning the management of business through effective budgeting and cashflow management, we cover the essentials of creating a budget and also monitoring cashflows.

However, before, in the subsequent chapters, we dive straight into the processes involved, below are some basic tips concerning the nature of budgets and the management of cashflows within business.

Purpose of Budgeting

In the context of business management, the purpose of budgeting includes the following three aspects:

- A forecast of income and expenditure (and thereby profitability)
- A tool for decision making
- A means to monitor business performance

Forecast of income and expenditure

Budgeting is a critically important part of the business planning process. Business owners and managers need to be able to predict whether a business will make a profit or not. The purpose of budgeting is basically to provide a model of how the business might perform, financially speaking, if certain strategies, events or plans are carried out.

In constructing a Business Plan, the manager attempts to forecast Income and Expenditure, and thereby profitability.

Tool for decision making

The purpose of budgeting is to provide a financial framework for the decision making process i.e. is the proposed course of action something we have planned for or not? In managing a business responsibly, expenditure must be tightly controlled. For example, when the budget for advertising has been fully expended, the decision on "can we spend money on advertising" is likely to be "no".

Monitoring business performance

The purpose of budgeting is to enable the **actual** business performance to be measured against the **forecast** business performance i.e. is the business living up to our expectations. See below for a sample budget spreadsheet. In the example below, "variance" is the difference between budgeted expenditure and actual expenditure.

Fig 1 Sample budget spreadsheet

	A	E	F	G	H
1		Budget 30 Apr 19	Actual 30 Apr 19	Variance £	Variance %
2	**Expenditure**				
3	Advertising & Promotion	£1,466.67	£200,00	£1,266.67	86%
4	Bank Charges	£166.67	£395.50	-£228.83	-137%
5	Photocopying & Print	£433.33	£566.30	-£132.97	-31%
6	Postage	£666.67	£1,153,40	-£486.73	-73%
7	Rent	£1,333.33	£1,000.00	£333.33	25%
8	Repairs &Renewals	£333.33	£225.00	£108.33	33%
9	Salaries	£18,333.33	£18,333.30	£0.03	0%
10	Stationery & Computer	£5000.00	£628.90	£128.90	-26%
11	Telephone	£1,000.00	£1,666,00	£666.00	-67%
12	12. **Total**	**£24,233.33**	**£24,167.40**	**£65.93**	**0%**

Budgeting Principles

For those who have the task of developing budgets or to be involved in the process of developing budgets, it is important to have a good knowledge of budgeting principles that can make the difference to the financial health of the organisation. Failure to engage in sound budgeting processes ranks as one of the main reasons why companies and organisations fail.

Be conservative not optimistic

The first principle of budgeting is to avoid budgeting on the basis that everything will turn out as expected. Be very cautious about optimistic forecasts. Try to build in a safety factor by tending to underestimate your income and overestimate your expenses. There will always be unexpected events and therefore a common strategy in developing a budget is to insert an additional expense called "contingencies". This item in the expense budget is an insurance policy against the unforeseen.

Team work and consultation

One of the most important principles of budgeting is that it requires teamwork and consultation. Although one person may be responsible for the overall compilation of the budget, one person should not be responsible for all the work involved. The task of budgeting should be split and allocated among those individuals who have the best chance of knowing what expenditure is likely to be needed and what income it is reasonable to expect. Involvement by many people in budgeting might slow the process down, but the answer is far more likely to be accurate and dependable.

Allow plenty of time

Budgeting is not an activity that is completed in a few hours. A good budget may be worked on for several weeks, if not months, adding and changing figures as new information comes to light. For this reason, budgeting is often seen as an iterative (repetitious) process. The budgeting process is lengthy because much research and consultation has to be carried out before people involved in the process can be confident of the figures they supply. (The process gets simpler the smaller the organisation-our assumptions throughout the book are based on a medium size business)

It is very important that the author(s) of the budget strive to produce documents that can be read and understood by anyone. If budget workings are unclear and figures are not clearly labelled even the author will, as time passes, have trouble understanding where the figures come from and how the calculations were made.

It should be assumed that budgeting workings will be:

- Circulated to many different people who may have lower levels of financial literacy
- Useful in a year's time when the budgeting process begins again. Unless workings are well labelled it may be difficult to remember.

Provide Training

Ensure people who have a significant role in the budgeting process have a reasonable understanding of the principles of budgeting, how it relates to the strategic and operational plans, and how everyone must live with the consequences of the finalised budget in the year ahead. Training need only be a single meeting in which those who have experience of budgeting provide knowledge to others involved who are less experienced.

Get Sign Off

Another one of the important principles of budgeting is to ensure that all persons formally involved in the budgeting process agree to the final version of the budget. This agreement by those involved is often referred to as the "Sign Off". In other words, those involved add their signature to the final budget. This ensures that there will be no argument later about who agreed to what.

Cashflow and Business

When it comes to the financial management of any business, it's often said that Cash Is King. Whether your business is growing or struggling, managing your cash flow effectively is absolutely essential, and for many, it's the key to business survival. You've probably heard the statistic that over 60% of businesses are still profitable, but just ran out of cash.

If you've used a lot of your working capital, you may come up against a cash crunch that prevents you from paying suppliers, buying materials and even paying salaries. The time delay between the time you have to pay your suppliers and the time you receive money from your customers is the problem, and the solution is cash flow management.

That's why it's critical to maintain a level of working capital that allows you to make it through those crunch times and continue to operate the business. Simply put, cash flow management means delaying outlays of cash as long as possible while encouraging your customers to pay it as quickly as possible.

Important Cash Flow Basics

So, what is cash flow? It's basically the movement of funds in and out of your business. Typically, businesses track cash flow either weekly, monthly or quarterly. There are essentially two kinds of cash flows:

- *Positive cash flow:* This occurs when the cash entering into your business from sales, accounts receivable, etc. is more than the amount of the cash leaving your businesses through accounts payable, monthly expenses, employee salaries, etc.
- *Negative cash flow:* This occurs when your outflow of cash is greater than your incoming cash.
- This generally means trouble for a business, but there are steps you can take to fix the negative cash flow problem and get into a positive zone

Profit Does Not Equal Good Cash Flow

You can't just look at your profit and loss statement (P&L) and get a grip on your cash flow. Many other financial figures feed into factoring your cash flow, including accounts receivable, stock, accounts payable, capital expenditures, taxation and VAT.

Find Out Your Breakeven Point

You should know when your business will become profitable, not because it will affect your cash flow — because it won't — but because it gives you an early goal to strive for and a ready-made target for projecting future cash flow. Negative cash flow and negative profits make for a grim combination. Focus your efforts on managing your cash flow with an eye toward reaching that moment when you realize your first profits.

You Can't Control What You Don't Measure

Finding out the amount of working capital a business needs to operate is the first step. You need to answer questions like:

- How much stock do I need to hold?
- How many invoices are overdue?
- How much cash is tied up in work in progress?
- How long does it take from paying our suppliers for the materials to extracting cash from the customers?

Your bookkeeper, accountant, accounting software and even spreadsheets can help you anticipate inflows and outflows of money over a period of time.

How To Fix Cash Flow Problem In Your Business – 5 Tips

Now that you have a fair idea about cash flow basics, lets see how you find solutions to cash flow problems:

1) Short-Term Financing

Short-term financing, such as a line of credit, can be used to make emergency purchases or to bridge the gap between payables and receivables. Many banks issue business credit cards that you can use to pay your vendors.

2) Long-Term Financing

Large asset purchases such as equipment and real estate should usually be financed with long-term loans rather than with your working capital. This allows you to spread the payments over the average life of the assets. You'll be paying interest, but you'll have preserved your working capital for business operations.

3) Speed Up Recovery Of Receivables

Bill early, collect quickly. To guard against late payments, bill as early as possible and make those invoices as clear and as detailed as possible. It may also be worth changing other billing practices such as invoice frequency. Instead of waiting until the end of the month, generate an invoice as soon as the goods or services are delivered.

For big orders, you may want to consider progressive invoicing while you manufacture the goods or deliver the service. For example, you can ask for a deposit with the order and then a percentage of the payment at various agreed upon milestones.

It's easy to lose track and then neglect to follow up on an overdue account. Experience shows that the longer you remain out of contact with a customer, the less likely you are to recover the amount owed. You can even consider offering discounts to customers who pay their bills rapidly.

Also, make it as easy as possible for your customers to pay you. For example, you can add a payment link on your invoice so that your customers can pay using a credit card.

Liquidate Cash Tied Up With Assets.

Do you have equipment you no longer use or stock that's becoming obsolete? Consider selling it to generate quick cash. Idle, obsolete, and non-working equipment takes up space and ties up capital which might be used more productively. Equipment that has been owned for a longer period will usually have a book value equal to its salvage value or less, so a sale might result in a taxable gain. This gain should be reported on your tax filings. If you have to sell below the book value, however, you will incur a tax loss, which can be used to offset other profits of the company.

Excess stock can quickly become obsolete and worthless as customer requirements change and new materials are introduced. Consider selling any stock which is unlikely to be used over the next 12 months unless the costs to retain it are minimal and the proceeds from a sale would be negligible.

5) Delay Your Payables

This may sound obvious but its often neglected. Unless there's a worthwhile incentive for you to pay early, figure out how late you can pay your vendors without risking late fees or harming your relationship. This keeps the cash in your account and out of your vendor's until it absolutely has to be there.

Best Practices For Managing A Healthy Cash Flow:

We've seen how you can quickly fix your cash flow problems using the tips mentioned above. However, its important to continuously maintain a healthy cashflow in your business or startup. You can:

1) Identify Business Risks & Prepare In Advance

There are many risks involved in running a business, and serious challenges should be expected at some point in the future. You need to consider a number of scenarios such as "What if that big order suddenly comes in?"; "What if a big order is cancelled?" or "What if that important client goes missing while still owing me money?" This kind of risk analysis can become part of your cash-flow budgeting process.

2) Have a Separate Bank Account For Your Business

A common mistake associated with running a business – especially among start-ups – is mixing business and personal bank accounts and credit cards. Since initial financing often comes from the owner's personal savings, it's easy to see how that can happen.

It's strongly advised to have a separate bank account for your business. You can ask your bank to issue a credit card, make business-related purchases on that card and pay using your company account. Most credit cards provide management reports that detail the types of purchases made over the month and over the past year. This type of information can then be used in your cash flow budget for the next year.

3) Always Keep Buffer Money

Once you find out the breakeven point as discussed further on, you must ensure your business has enough cash to fund your working capital needs. It's advised to keep three months worth of outgoings in the bank for a rainy day. That may be a thing of the past, but if that's the case with you, make sure you have a buffer of some sort, either personal funds available or an overdraft or revolving credit facility.

4) Implement A Better System To Manage Cash Flow

Many businessmen procrastinate before invoicing customers. Some do not invoice as soon as they deliver the product or services or do it just at the month end. Many do not even know how much is owed to them by their customers or how much they owe to suppliers. If you are one of them, its time to start implementing an efficient process to manage cash flow. You can use a simple spreadsheet or an accounting software. But it is important to have some system in place.

5) Cut Costs, Control Cash Outflows

the best way to control cash flow is to stay on top of your expenses. When we start making profits, we often tend to ignore the cost cutting opportunities. Unmanaged outflow could be a silent business killer.

6) Keep Your Cash Growing

Keep your cash balances in interest-earning accounts, which are available at most banks. In some cases, you might encounter a minimum balance requirement. However, since interest rates on these accounts are often lower than those of savings accounts, consider keeping the bulk of your funds in higher-paying accounts, then transferring funds to meet the minimum balance requirement in your interest-bearing cheque account (plus the total payments due that week or month).

The above are general outlines of efficient and effective control of business through the utilisation of budgets and cashflow management tools. The whole process is down to effective scrutiny of all aspects of the business.

The whole idea of this book is not to confuse people at the outset with complex accounting practices as they relate to business but to highlight the fundamental processes of creating budgets and also monitoring cashflows.

In the following chapters we will first look briefly at the principles of basic bookkeeping and then go through the basic stages of creating budgets and monitoring cashflows. A basic knowledge of bookkeeping is fundamental to good business management.

****

2.
AN INTRODUCTION TO BASIC BOOKKEEPING

Chapter 2

An Introduction to Basic Bookkeeping

In Chapter 1 we looked at budgets and cashflows generally. In Chapter 2, we look closely at the basic elements of bookkeeping, which forms one of the day-to-day activities of running a business, whether sole trader, limited company or partnership. We look at what information should be kept, the advantages of a good bookkeeping system, the recording of information, and also give examples of how to record transactions. This will provide the backdrop for the following chapters which deal with the processes of setting budgets and monitoring cashflows.

Business activities of a company or enterprise

Your business activities, in common with all businesses, will consist of selling goods and/or services. At the same time you will have to spend money on behalf of the business, on the purchase or rent of premises, wages or salaries, raw materials, equipment, stationery etc. etc. in order to conduct business. *The main point is that every business transaction generates a financial transaction, all of which must be recorded in books of account on an ongoing basis.* It is a fundamental management requirement that this be done on a regular basis, at a minimum once a week. Leave it much longer, and sooner or later an iron law of accounting will come into operation. You will have mislaid a financial record or simply forgotten to request one or issue one. When you do get around to up-dating the books, they won't balance. Unless you can discover the error before the end of the financial year your accountant, if you have one, will be faced with the task of reconciling "incomplete records", which he or she will enjoy because of the professional challenge but which costs you more money for more of his/her time.

What information must be kept?

As a minimum you must keep records of the following:

i) All the invoices raised (or rendered) on behalf of the business, An invoice is a legal document and it constitutes a formal demand for money. It must provide enough information to identify the business which sent it, who it was sent to, what it is for and whether VAT is payable. These invoices should be numbered sequentially.

See further on for an example invoice.

ii) All Purchase invoices received, and listed i.e. those demands made on your business for the payment of money.

iv) Wages and salaries paid, and to whom; Income tax and NI contributions paid over to the Tax authorities. Also, pension contributions.

v) All chequebook stubs, paying-in slips/books, counterfoils of petty cash vouchers, business bank account statements. Without these you cannot compile your books of account.

vi) A full record of VAT, whether paid by or paid to the business.

These records will be kept, initially, in main, or prime, books of account, as we will see.

The advantages of a good bookkeeping system for your business
Following on from this, you need a bookkeeping system that mirrors your day-to-day activity. The fundamental purpose of a bookkeeping system is :

a) To provide accurate information sufficient to assess whether you are managing the business at a profit or a loss, or whether the business is solvent i.e. is there enough cash available in the business to pay all the outstanding liabilities on demand? The right information of the right kind at the right time is a vital management tool. Good management means making informed decisions of the right kind at the right time based on information that is true and therefore trustworthy.

b) To provide the information required for correct assessments of VAT and Income Tax, so as to avoid financial penalties (and possibly a suspect reputation) for incorrect and/or late payments. HM Revenue and Customs keeps records for seven years. Your accountant will need the best information in order to minimise your tax liabilities, unless of course you decide to submit a statement of income to your Inspector of Taxes without recourse to an accountant. In any event the Inspector will require a calculation of your Income from the business in the form of an Income and Expenditure Account for each trading year.

c) To monitor the behaviour of the business over time by reference to financial summaries "at a glance". You don't need to remember for example how many bricks were sold in your building materials business in this financial year compared with last year. The comparison that matters is the financial one with reference to the value of those transactions.

How to record the information you need

There are, basically, three methods of bookkeeping, outlined below. These are the:

- **Proprietary system** usually used by a small trader or sole trader;
- **The single entry system** (also known as the analysed cash book system) which is most commonly used and which entails keeping books of account, the information from which is transferred to;
- **The Double entry system** to build up books of account. Which one to choose will depend largely on the type and size of business you have established. Take advice from a business adviser or accountant if you are unsure as to which is the best one for your needs.

Most businesses nowadays will use computing software for speed and accuracy, which will encompass all of the above systems.

a) Proprietary systems.

These are best suited for sole traders in cash transaction types of business, e.g. jobbing builders, market traders or some small shopkeepers. This type of business requires daily record keeping, often including till-rolls for the cash till and offers a simple method of control over finances. In reality, most small business people would use a spreadsheet or software. If you are using a manual system a number of pre-printed stationery books are available at business bookshops. Select one that allows you enough space to record all that needs recording. Worked examples are set out at the beginning of each book to show you how to keep cash records and the bank position, which can be calculated by following the instructions included. Cash businesses are more vulnerable than other types for the following reasons: -

i) It is far easier to lose or misplace paperwork. Therefore it is easier to lose control and lose money. It is more difficult to plan for the future.

ii) It is far more difficult to separate the cash that belongs in the business from the cash belonging to the proprietor.

iii) HMRC pays far closer attention to cash businesses because of the greater scope for "creative accounting" and tax evasion.

b) The Cash Book System (single entry).

This is perhaps the most common method used by small businesses selling mostly on credit, with perhaps some cash sales. It relies on the Single Entry system of bookkeeping, where each entry is, as the name implies, made once only, and all entries are made in one (of a number) of books. (see further on for examples).

The cashbook is the "bible" of the business where business transactions are initially recorded from source documents such as invoices, receipts, bank transfers etc. It allows "at a glance" analysis because it is arranged on a columnar basis, showing how much has been received into the business, when and from where, how much of each receipt is attributable to VAT and therefore how much is the net amount belonging to the business. At some point the entries from the accounts books will find their way onto ledgers, through the double entry system of accounting.

Although most people or organisations now use software systems, for the purposes of learning, before you can understand accounting software you need to understand the accounting process, which is why we are laying out a manual system of bookkeeping. There will usually be six account books as follows:

- The Sales Book-this will record credit sales (or sales on credit)

- The corresponding purchases book which will record purchases on credit

- The Cash Book, or cash receipts book, which records cash received from customers and any other sources.

- The Cheque payments book which records payments made by cheque or debits from the bank account belonging to the business
- The petty cash book which, as its name suggests will record all minor cash expenses going out of the business
- Finally, a general book which records any transactions not made by the other books.

Example 1-The sales account book

Peters Building Supplies Ltd Sales account Book					
Date	Ref	Total	sales @ 20%	10%	VAT
14/11/19	Inv 32	£750	600		£150
19/11/2019	Inv 33	£300	£240		£60
22/11/19	Inv 34	£1500	£1200		£300
Total		£2550	£2040		£510

As mentioned, the Sales account book records sales made on credit. The source documents are the sales invoices, as per the above example. Most business will make sales on credit, usually setting their terms at 28 days, or whatever they have agreed with the business involved. You will see that the VAT rate is set at 20% although an extra column is set at 10% for a different VAT rate if applicable. By maintaining your day books this way you are keeping a running total of VAT charged.

Example 2-The Purchases Account Book

Peters Building Supplies Ltd					
Purchases account Book					
Date	Ref	Total	sales @ 20%	10%	VAT
14/11/19	16	£400	320		£80
16/11/19	17	£550	430		110
22/11/19	18	£760	608		152
Total		£1710	£1358		£342

The Purchases Account Book records purchases made on credit. The source documents are the suppliers invoices. You will see that the VAT rate is set at 20% although an extra column is set at 10% for a different VAT rate if applicable. The Purchase Account Book is similar to the Sales account Book however the reference column will show the invoice number of the suppliers invoice

Example 3-Cash Receipt Book (overleaf)

Peters Building Supplies Ltd							
Cash Receipts Book							
Date	Detail	Ref	Total	20%	10%	MISC	VAT Paid In

The Cash Receipts Book, as the name suggest, records all cash received by a business, which is usually paid into a bank account. Sources of cash into a business would usually be from cash sales, cash received from customers allowed credit. There will also be miscellaneous cash. Cash sales are usually made to customers who do not have credit, such as the general public.

In the layout of a typical Cash Sales Book above. you will see columns as follows:

- Date,
- Detail of sale,
- The reference number assigned to it
- Total amount,
- VAT at two rates
- A Miscellaneous column which details odd sums

- VAT amount
- The amount paid into the bank.

Although two entries have been made, during the course of the business many more entries will be made with the running totals adjusting accordingly.

Example 4-Cheque/bank transfer Payment Books

Peters Building Supplies Ltd

Cheque payments

Date	Detail	Chq ref	Total	Creditors	Utilities	Wages	Phone	VAT	Misc
17/10	M Ltd	621326	400	400					
Total			400	400					

Different businesses will have different ways of laying out cheque payment books. The payment may also be a bank transfer so the cheque ref could also be a transfer ref. The above is pretty standard and the book is laid out as follows:

- Date
- Detail-to whom cheque payment made
- The cheque number which helps you to track payments

- The total
- A Creditors column to show that the payment was made to a trade creditor
- Whether the payment was for a utility such as electricity or gas
- Wages
- Phone
- Any VAT element
- A Miscellaneous column for any miscellaneous payment

Again, I have indicated one payment but in reality there would be many with running totals.

Example 5-Petty Cash Book

Peters Building Supplies Ltd

Petty cash book

Date			Paid out	Item	Total		Teas	Office	Other
17/10	Balance	75	17/10	Sugar	2.50	2.50			
18/10	Cheque	£30	18/10	cleaner	£15		£15		
Total		**£105**			**£17.50**	**£17.50**			

Petty Cash Books run on what is known as the imprest system. This basically means that a certain petty cash balance is maintained and topped up at regular intervals. The second column shows a balance of £75 topped up by a cheque of £30. The columns show amount spent, on what and the overall totals spent. Of course businesses can keep what form of petty cash record they want as long as a clear record is maintained.

Example 6- The General Day Book or Journal

The general day book is the final day book and it records transactions that are not recorded elsewhere. The journal is typically used to enter any corrections to minor errors made in the other day books.

Peters building supplies Ltd			
Journal			
Date	Account	Debit	Credit
17/10/2019	Write off bad debt Foreman Ltd	£2,000	£2,000

This journal simply shows the date and columns for the narrative explaining what the entry is related to plus debit and credit. In this case, we have a bad debt that will not be paid. This can't be recorded in any other day book so goes in the general journal.

Invoices

It is important that you are consistent with the types of invoice that you use and to make sure that they are sequentially numbered when they are entered onto the appropriate account book

Example Invoice

INVOICE

From: Peters Building Supplies Ltd   Invoice number 32

    16 Merrygate

    Merrytown

    Anywhere

To: David James Building- 32 Anywhere

Date: 14/11/2019

VAT Registration number 12345678

Goods	£600
VAT	£150
Total:	**£750**

With Thanks

Payable within 28 days

Of course, businesses can use any design they wish as long as you have all of the important information, such as VAT number, date, amount, from whom and to whom.

VAT

It is very important indeed that clear and accurate records are kept of VAT transactions, such as sales and receipts. In addition, your invoices, if you are VAT registered, should always indicate your VAT number. The examples above enable you to record VAT as a running total.

The Double Entry System

This method of recording accounts builds on the maintenance of account books detailed above and, as we shall see in the next chapter, relies on ledgers, or **separate books of account** for each type of transaction. All entries in the account books are recorded in sub-accounts called 'ledgers' in order to differentiate financial information'.

Computerised Accounting Systems

Computerised accounting, using accounting software involves making use of computers and software to record, store and analyse financial data. As explained, although most businesses now use software to provide an accounting system, it is essential to understand the main principles underlying accounting for business before using accounting packages. This is what this book is about.

A computerized accounting system brings with it many advantages that are unavailable to manual accounting systems. Quick books, heavily advertised on TV is one such system but there are many others, such as Sage. The numerous advantages of using computerized accounting software are:

Automation: Since all the calculations are handled by the software, computerized accounting eliminates many of the mundane and time-consuming processes associated with manual accounting. For example, once issued, invoices are processed automatically making accounting less time-consuming.

Accuracy: This accounting system is designed to be accurate to the tiniest detail. Once the data is entered into the system, all the calculations, including additions and subtractions, are done automatically by software.

Data Access: Using accounting software, it becomes much easier for different individuals to access accounting data outside of the office, securely.

Reliability: Because the calculations are so accurate, the financial statements prepared by computers are highly reliable.

Scalability: When your company grows, the amount of accounting necessary not only increases but becomes more complex. With computerized accounting, everything is kept straightforward because sifting through data using software is easier than sifting through a pile of papers.

Speed: Using accounting software, the entire process of preparing accounts becomes faster. Furthermore, statements and reports can be generated instantly at the click of a button. Managers do not have to wait for hours, even days, to lay their hands on an important report.

Security: The latest data can be saved and stored in offsite locations so it is safe from natural and man-made disasters like fires, floods, arson and terrorist attacks. In case of a disasters, the system can be quickly restored on other computers.

Cost-effective: Since using computerized accounting is more efficient than paper-based accounting, and work will be done faster and time will be saved.

Visuals: Viewing your accounts using a computer allows you to take advantage of the option to view your data in different formats. You can view data in tables and using different types of charts.

Now read a summary of the main points from Chapter 2 overleaf

****

Summary of Main Points From Chapter 2.

- Your business activities, in common with all businesses, will consist of selling goods and/or services. At the same time you will have to spend money on behalf of the business, on the purchase or rent of premises, wages or salaries, raw materials, equipment, stationery etc. etc. in order to conduct business.

- The main point is that every business transaction generates a financial transaction, all of which must be recorded in books of account on an ongoing basis. .

- Following on from this, you need a bookkeeping system that mirrors your day-to-day activity.

- The method of bookkeeping used will depend on the type of business involved. The most common bookkeeping system used is the single entry (analysed) system-which in turn builds up information for recording onto a double entry (Ledger) system.

****

3.

MANAGEMENT ACCOUNTING-BUDGETS AND CASHFLOWS GENERALLY- CREATING A BUDGET

Chapter 3

Management Accounting-Budgets and Cashflows Generally

Having looked at the elements of basic bookkeeping in Chapter 2, we will now turn to the main purpose of the book and examine the central role of budgets and cashflow tools, within the context of management accounting.

The profitability of a business is, in the main, the outcome of two elements:

- Tight control of overheads
- Correct pricing to ensure that the margin of profit is realistic.

Management Accounting

Management accounting produces information mainly for internal use by the company's management, primarily information relating to budget and cashflows but also more complex information. The information produced is generally more detailed than that produced for external use to enable effective organizational control and the fulfillment of the strategic aims and objectives of the business. Information may be in the form of budgets and forecasts, enabling an enterprise to plan effectively for its future or may include an assessment based on its past performance and results. The form and content of any report produced in the process is purely upon management's discretion.

As we have seen in the introduction, accurate forecasting, through the formulation of budgets and monitoring of cash flow is absolutely essential to the profitability of any business. Following on, we saw in chapter 2 that the maintenance of effective systems to record information is essential.

Control of Cash-flows into and out of a business

A smooth and regular cash flow, or the achievement of such involves:

- Making sure that a business is run profitably

- Payment control

- Utilisation of any available credit. This is of the utmost importance as the alternative is costly borrowing

- The attainment of correct stocking levels

Basically, money is vital to the life of any business and the forecasting of cash flow is essential in order to both measure the growth and direction of the business and to enable you to make strategic decisions at a given point in time. It is equally vital to ensure that sources of business finance are identified and readily available in times of increased need for capital.

Budgets

A budget is used, in both a business and personal sense, as a tool to **forecast expenditure** and to **monitor cash flow** at regular intervals. It is a plan expressed in quantitative terms and should be part of an ongoing business plan.

Budgets are necessary to enable you to plan what your business will do at given points in time.

All aspects of a business have to be defined and factored into a budget, which will usually run for the financial year of the business and be broken down into monthly elements in order to allow for an ongoing review of progress. An effective budget is also essential as a tool to enable you to deal with potential funders, such as bank managers.

The monitoring function of a carefully prepared budget can help you to identify certain trends and needs, such as the maintenance of stock levels and debtors. We will look at these processes further on in the book. An effective budget is both a guesstimate and, in certain areas, an accurate appraisal of expenditure.

Formulating budgets

Budgets are effective tools, both in forecasting the pattern of business and also as a tool for development. For budgets to be of any real use they should be split up into monthly periods. This is very important if the nature of your business is affected by seasonal trends. As the months pass any adjustments can be made in the light of variations and can be fed into the ongoing budget. (see fig 1 chapter 1).

Cash flow considerations

Central to any budget setting is the need to estimate cash flow and to ensure that your projections are adequately sourced. It is no good having a production budget which anticipates an increase of 50% in production if the money is not there to finance it. We will be looking at cash flows in more depth a little later on.

To re-cap, the key steps involved in budget preparation are as follows:

- The period that should be covered by your budget has to be ascertained. Usually, the period will correspond to the financial year of a business. It is also necessary to decide the periods into which the budget will be divided, i.e. 12 monthly periods

- Forecast activity levels and the income from trading and other sources for each of the periods. The forecast should reflect the fact that income streams may be irregular, as is the nature for some businesses

- When the level of sales has been determined for each period it is then necessary to ascertain the cost of sales

- The next step is to forecast the level of each of the overhead expenses.

- Finally, confirm that your plan fits into the cash budget.

Having arrived at the figures you will be in a position to produce a monthly budgeted profit and loss account like the one shown overleaf in fig 2.

*

Fig 2. Example monthly budgeted Profit and Loss account

Items	January			February	
	Budget	Actual	(Variance)	Budget	Actual (V)
Sales					
Direct costs					
Purchases of goods					
Wages					
Stock					
Cost of goods sold					
Gross profit					
Overheads					
Motor expenses					
Repairs and renewals					
Telephone charges					
Printing and stationary					
Heating and lighting					
Insurance					
Rates					
Bank charges and interest					
Professional fees					
Sundry expenses					
Depreciation					
Net profit					

The budget will have an actuals column and also a budget column plus a variance column. This will enable you to see, on a monthly basis, the level of expenditure and the deviation from the budget. If there are significant variations between the actual and budget column then there will be several considerations:

- It is essential to consider why the business is not performing as you have forecasted. Where are things going wrong, if they are going wrong
- The budget may need to be revised for the rest of the year, based on the variations, which may involve management decisions related to expenditure

As we will see, this procedure of review is extended automatically to the cash flow forecast. There are key considerations for any one involved in budget setting. These are as follows:

- The quality and accuracy of any budget will depend on the assumptions made by the person/people involved in the budget process. Do not be sloppy and lazy when it comes to forecasting.
- Be rigorous and honest in your assumptions. The most important thing to realise when setting the budget is that, in a lot of cases, it will be essential to study the previous year's performance in order to be able to set a future budget.

- The budget is very much a management tool and the performance against budget at the end of each period is a crucial indicator for the future.
- Cash is the lifeblood-business activity totally depends on it and it is vital that this side is under control.
- The activities of one particular period in time will reflect and modify the next period.

Now read the main points from Chapter 3 overleaf.

****

Summary of Main Points From Chapter 3.

- The profitability of a business is, in the main, the outcome of two elements: Tight control of overheads; Correct pricing to ensure that the margin of profit is realistic.

- Management accounting produces information mainly for internal use by the company's management.

- Money is vital to the life of any business and the forecasting of cash flow is essential in order to both measure the growth and direction of the business and to enable you to make strategic decisions at a given point in time.

- A budget is used, in both a business and personal sense, as a tool to **forecast expenditure** and to **monitor cash flow** at regular intervals.

****

Chapter 4

The Process of Setting Budgets

Whilst accounts show what has happened over a predetermined period of time, the budget will, or should, show what will happen in the near future. Budgets are essential tools in forecasting the pattern of business and also as a tool for development.

As we have discussed, for budgets to be of any real use they should be split up into monthly periods. As the months pass any adjustments can be made in the light of variations and can be fed into the ongoing budget.

The putting together of a detailed budget involves a process which is linked. Key links in the budget setting process are outlined below:

- Sales budget-production budget

You need to consider the production capacity when setting the sales budget. It is essential that accuracy is achieved in this area as it is no good budgeting for production of goods which exceeds your real capacity.

- Sales budget-cost of sales

There are close links between these two budgets. The selling price has to reflect the costs of production and an element for profit. You will need an idea of the sales volume when setting this budget as the costs of production go down as actual production goes up.

- Overheads-sales budgets

The overheads of the business will be incurred whatever the level of turnover. However, the cost of the overheads will need to be carried by the sales of the product. The lower the volume of sales the more overhead cost has to be absorbed in the selling price of each item.

In practice the overhead expenses are often apportioned back to the cost of sales on a cost centre basis. This is affected by the size of the organisation and its diversity. All these elements grouped together will enable you to ascertain the budgeted gross and net profits for the period. In a small organisation the process of budgeting will be invariably easier as there will be less considerations. However, the larger and more departmentalised an organisation becomes the greater the need for co-operation between people and departments.

Format of the Budget

The format of a budget should, broadly, follow the profit and loss account, although it will also include items of a capital nature. The preparation of any budget will usually be more detailed than the profit and loss account.

Costs involved in business

Some expenses in business are fixed and some are variable. There are also direct and indirect costs involved in the production process. Most direct costs are variable whilst the indirect costs are usually fixed. Direct costs are those associated with the production of the product itself whilst indirect costs are concerned with the overall running of a business.

Fixed and variable costs

If we look at the elements of fixed and variable costs, then it can be seen that raw materials to produce a product will be variable. The higher the level of overall activity the more variable the material costs. Energy for production will correspondingly vary as will transport. The logic is that the more that a business produces the more variable will the overall costs be.

However, other costs, such as rent or rates and business rates will not vary with the highs and lows of production. These costs will remain stable, they will be the same even if you did not produce a thing. The costs of salaries are fixed and identifiable and are therefore fixed.

Semi-variable costs

Some costs are not regarded as truly variable. Key examples may be labour and machinery. When production reaches a certain limit it may be necessary to take on more labour and invest in more machinery. This will obviously come into effect with increased production and this is why labour and machinery has to be identified as semi-variable in nature. Particular attention should be paid to this area as incorrect forecasting can have a detrimental effect on business planning.

Selling expenses

The size of a sales force will clearly be affected by the levels of activity within the business. If interest is shown in a product then it may be necessary to increase your sales force, if appropriate. This is also a consideration to take on board.

Budgeting sales income

The top line on the profit and loss account is usually the sales income. Very often it is the sales figure that heads the budget and everything else is fitted in. If you have been in business for a while then past trends can influence your future budget. It will be essential to look at the number of units sold and also the values of those units.

The unit values decided upon by yourself will very much reflect the type of business that you are engaged in. For example, a publisher would measure units in terms of individual books, a window cleaner individual houses and so on.

Who should carry out the sales forecasting?

If you work alone then the answer is simple-you will do the forecasting. If the organisation is larger then all departments will usually have a hand in the forecasting process. It is absolutely essential that the process is well co-ordinated.

Creating the budget-A Publishing Company

From research carried out you have identified that the sales of your product will be along the following lines:

Product	Unit sales per month	
Books-paperback	£ 750	
Books-hardback	£350	
Magazines	£450	
The prices of the products are likely to be:		
Books-paperback	£ 7.99	
Books-hardback	£ 9.99	
Magazines	£3.50	
Therefore the monthly sales figures would look like this:		
Product Units	Price	Value
Books-paperback 750	£7.99	£ 5992.50
Books-hardback 350	£9.99	£3496.50
Magazines 459	£3.50	£15.75
	Value,	£11064

If your business has seasonal trends then it will be necessary to produce separate figure for each month in order to maintain an accurate picture.

Arriving at price-price budgeting

You will usually have a keen idea of the market and corresponding prices for your goods. However, you also need to sell your goods at a profit and you therefore need to establish how much the product has cost in order to ascertain your profit margins.

When trying to establish the actual cost of production it is necessary to take into account the fact that there are two types of costs-direct and indirect costs. As we have seen, direct costs are those incurred directly in producing the product and they include materials, wages and other direct costs such as energy.

Indirect costs are those costs which do not relate directly to production, including costs of selling and marketing, rent, rates and insurance.

Example - Direct and indirect costs:

Direct Costs	Indirect costs
Materials	Overheads
	Admin + labour
Direct Labour	Selling and marketing
	Insurance-building repairs
Production costs	Depreciation

Having projected your sales and anticipated income, then you will need to set this off against the actual costs of production. Remember the actual cost of production will include all costs, direct and indirect. Therefore, if you are producing books, and you both manufacture and sell the product and the out turn price of a paperback is £7.99, this will be set off against the actual costs of production. For example:

Costs of production
Product-Paperback book
Print run 1000
Materials required

	£
	£
Paper 100 mts	Cost 150
Cover film	Cost 100
Bar code	Cost 9.99
Glue	Cost 20.00
	Total 279.99

Labour

4 persons @ £9.87 per hour for 15 hours £140.05

Overheads   £
Rent   per annum   5000

Rates		842
Light		600
Heating		1200
Transport		12500
	Total	15152

Based on the production of 50,000 units per annum

0.30p per unit times 1000 total 300

Therefore total costs of production are:

£720.04 for 1000 print run or 0.72p per unit.

The cost of distribution, which is carried out by an independent distributor, represents 55% of cover price (£7.99) which is £4.39.

Costs of production @ 0.72 per unit plus £4.39 distribution costs represents a cost of £5.11. This represents a profit so far of £2.88 per unit. Other costs, if they exist are the costs of sales, such as advertising and marketing.

However, assuming there are no other costs of sales then the actual cost to the publisher is £5.11 set off against the selling price of £7.99. The differential £2.88 represents profit of around 27% which is a respectable return on capital employed.

The cost of production including distributors costs produces a profit margin of £2.88. This is based on you having established that the market will pay £7.99 for your books. However, there may be situations when you are faced with the need to reduce prices in the face of fresh competition and price cutting. It may be that your competitor has produced a range of books which are similar to yours and is selling them at £5.99. You can go two ways here-maintain your prices and leave it to the consumer to discriminate or re-examine your pricing.

Reducing your product to £5.99 would have the effect of a loss of £2 per item which, when worked back would entail a loss of approximately 90pence per unit. If you were not prepared to tolerate this loss, or were in a position where you could not lose such an amount of money, then hard decisions have to be made. The overall costings would need to be re-examined to see if any extra savings could be made. For example, many overhead costs are fixed and an increase in overall production could reduce costs correspondingly.

*

Break even analysis

One technique widely employed in this situation is called break-even analysis. In the example of the book, not enough is lost, even with such a big price production by the competitor, to warrant the need for a break-even analysis. However, there will be situations depending on the nature of a business, where it will be necessary to establish at what point in production you reach a break even level.

As we discussed earlier, expenses can be split into fixed and variable costs. Fixed costs will include all the overheads such as rent and rates and insurance whilst variable costs are those incurred in production itself. The total costs of running the business are therefore the sum of the fixed costs and the variable costs during that period.

The more items produced, the higher the total cost but even if nothing is produced fixed costs will be incurred. Therefore, you will need to know the point of production at which you break even.

Calculating the break even point

Whenever you sell a product, part of the proceeds of sale will be used to meet variable costs-the costs of producing a specific item. The rest is applied towards the fixed costs and the remainder, if there is any, will be profit. The remainder, the profit, is referred as the contribution from the sale of the product.

	£
If a product sells for	7.99
And the variable costs are	2.89
The contribution is therefore	5.10

This means that for every unit sold you will receive £5.10 towards the business. If the fixed costs are £450 per week and you have sold 200 units you will have received £1020 contribution from the sales and be in profit. If however, you sell 89 units in that week you will receive £453.90 which will meet fixed costs and leave you in a break even situation.

You therefore have established that you need to sell 89 units in order to reach a position where you have broken even. Any less and you will be in a loss making situation, any more and your profit margin will begin to increase.

If as a result of reviewing your situation, you decide to reduce prices then you will need to revise your sales forecast

Internal budgeting-budgeting for expected overheads and capital items

So far we have examined the forecasting of the level of sales, the direct costs of the products and how to calculate the gross profit arising from selling products. We need now to look at the other expenses of the business.

Budgeting for overheads

We need to look at the indirect costs associated with business activity, more specifically overheads.

Overheads include:
- Rent and rates
- Salaries
- Pensions
- Stationary
- Telephone costs
- Travelling expenses
- Insurance
- Bank charges
- Entertaining
- Depreciation
- Accountancy, audit and legal fees

Rent and rates

If you are leasing a premises then the overheads associated with this are fixed and known, i.e. fixed annual rental, insurance, service charge if appropriate and business rates. If you own the premises outright then the costs will be minus rent. The only unforeseen costs associated with both leased and freehold property will be unexpected repair costs.

Salaries

Wages will include all other associated costs such as employers National Insurance Contributions, pension contributions if any and any other benefits. A global figure for the costs of labour has to be established. These costs can be easily understood throughout the year, as the only variation will be cost of living increases and the occasional increase in NI contributions.

Stationary

This particular item will cover all the costs of stationary throughout the business. It includes company letterheads, envelopes, copier paper and so on. This has to be seen against a backdrop of the previous year's expenditure and can be quite easily ascertained.

Telephone

There are two elements to telephone charges, telephone also including fax:

Rental

= *Quarterly line rental*

Calls

This area also has to be measured against the previous year's expenditure. It is an area that will vary depending on the levels of business. The only constant is the fact that whether business rises or falls the level of telephone activity is likely to remain constant. If you are losing business, calls will be made to potential customers. If your business activity has increased then the phone is likely to be used more.

A look at last year's quarterly bills and progress against budget should help you to arrive at a fairly accurate picture.

Travelling

This particular cost will vary widely from one business to another. Certain businesses require very little travel whilst others require extensive rail, air and road travel. Again, this cost will be influenced by the level of business and you should be able to ascertain the broad cost quite accurately.

Insurance

A business will need several different insurances. These include:

- Public liability
- Employers liability
- Building insurance
- Equipment insurance
- Consequential loss insurance
- Product insurance.

Obviously, the nature and type of your business will determine the types of insurance needed. These will be easily identified and the costs fixed.

Bank charges

Banks publish a list of their charges and they should be quantifiable. However, charges can be negotiated so there may be room for improvement in this area.

Entertaining

This particular item will vary depending on the nature and type of the business. Again, you know the needs of your business and the value of entertaining and the costs should be easily quantifiable.

Depreciation

This reflects the loss in the value of capital equipment. This is a revenue expense but has to be discussed further within the context of capital expenditure.

Accountancy and audit fees

The charges from your accountant can be fixed, i.e. one fee is payable or they can vary depending on the charging structure of the accountant used. In addition, the nature and type of service will vary, some companies will use an accountant for all its functions whilst others will use them only for preparation of end of years accounts. Again, you know the extent to which accountants are used within your company and also the likely charges. One other area to consider is that of selling and distribution and the expenses associated with these elements. These can include:

- Sales representatives salaries
- Commissions

- Travel expenses
- Sales office expenses
- Communications
- Accommodation
- Publicity (advertising)

And any other item associated with this area.

You should be in a position, having identified all the relevant cost areas to draw up an administration budget like the one shown on page 80.

Budgeting for capital items

The capital budget is every bit as important as the revenue budget. The revenue budget deals with the day to day running costs and income of the business, the capital budget will deal with the provision of capital items such as machinery, vehicles etc. The capital budget is of more relevance to cash flow than to revenue expenditure and we will be looking at this at little later.

Capital expenditure has an impact on profitability in two key ways:

- By increasing the depreciation charge
- By increasing the amount of interest payable as a result of borrowed money

The timing of capital expenditure can have a dramatic effect on cash flow of a business. It is important to time the acquisition of capital items with cash flow into the business as this will decrease reliance on the need to borrow or to spend much needed capital and find your business in trouble.

See overleaf for an example of an administration budget and an overall revenue budget.

Example of an administration budget

Period 12 Months to 31ˢᵗ March

Previous years actual	Current	Budget
Materials		
Stationary		
Other		
Salaries and Wages/Pensions		
Management		
Clerical		
Cleaners		
Other		
Expenses		
Rent and rates		
Telephone		
Postage		
Travelling		
Entertaining		
Insurance		
Bank Charges		
Audit and accountancy		
Subscriptions		
Depreciation		
Other		

Example of an overall revenue budget
The period 12 months to 31st March

	Products			
	Type A	Type B	Type C	Total
Sales				
Cost of sales				
Contribution to profit				
Selling and distribution overheads				
Administration overheads				
Total Overheads				
Budgeted profit				

Now read the key points from Chapter 4 overleaf.

****

Summary of Main Points From Chapter 4.

- The format of a budget should, broadly, follow that of the profit and loss account. The preparation of any budget will usually be more detailed than the profit and loss account.

- It is absolutely essential that the budget setting process is well co-ordinated.

- One important element in the budget setting process, depending on the type and nature of the business, is that of arriving at a break-even point, through carrying out a break even analysis.

- All elements of the business must be included in the budget setting process. A budget must incorporate all the interrelationships between different activities.

****

5.

MANAGING CASHFLOW

Chapter 5

Cash Flow Management

A cash flow forecast deals with transactions at the time of payment. Cash does not necessarily accrue at the same time as a sale takes place. The sale may take place in August of one year but, depending on what credit agreements you have in place with your customers, payments may arrive up to 3 months later. There are many stories of companies, particularly large companies, who withhold payments for 6 months or more.

Once you have prepared a budgeted profit and loss account it is then essential to review the cash situation of the business to ensure the finance will be there to make the business possible. Sales are the heart that pumps money into the business. Cash flow is payment for those sales, and this must be very closely regulated.

The cash flow forecast
Quite simply, a cash flow forecast will measure the flow and movements of cash. A bank will absolutely insist on seeing a well-

prepared forecast. Most banks will provide a standard cash flow form like the one overleaf to assist those who are not so experienced in these matters. As with the budget, the actual timeframe covered by the cash flow forecast is very important. As with the budget, a cash flow forecast from month to month is the norm. This enables you to see the flow of cash in finer detail and enables you to plan.

If your business is of a certain type it might be possible to produce a cash flow forecast covering longer than the standard one-year period. This very much depends on your product and the nature of your sales. However, the longer period a cash flow forecast covers the less accurate it is likely to be.

If you look at the standard cash flow form on page 89 you will see that it is divided into the following parts:
- Dates covering the length of time relevant to the forecast
- Receipts
- Payments
- Opening bank balance
- Closing bank balance

The closing balance for one period will be the opening balance of the next period.

Looking at the headings on the form overleaf, it can be seen that income has been divided into:

- Cash sales

- Debtors

- Other income

Forecasting cash flow

The first heading, cash sales, entails sales where cash is received immediately. There is no credit period involved. Certain businesses are (part) cash businesses (now usually accepting contactless payments as well). Shops, cafes, public houses are all in the position where they receive some cash over the counter. This is as opposed to the business, which invoices for its sales. Cash includes cash, cheque, visa and so on. If you have a detailed monthly operating budget then it should be relatively easy to work out monthly cash flow.

Debtors

On a cash flow forecast we are concerned with cash transactions (inputs). The sale and when it is made is not relevant. This is more relevant to your operating budget. The most important entry will be the date that you expect to receive payment for that particular sale. This can be measured with some certainty by your agreed credit agreements with your customers. The important thing is to monitor the cash flow on a monthly basis.

It may well be that your customers will exceed the period of credit given to them and that you need to adjust your cash flow forecast as you go along.

Example cash flow forecast overleaf.

Business   **Period Covered**

Receipts	Month Budget Actual	Month Budget Actual	Month Budget Actual	Month Budget Actual
Cash Sales				
Cash from debtors				
Capital introduced				
Total receipts (a)				
Payments				
Payments to creditors				
Salaries/wages				
Rent/rates/water				
Insurance				
Repairs/renewals				
Heat/light/power				
Printing/stationary				
Motor and travel				
Telephone				
Professional fees				
Capital payments				
Interest and				

charges				
Other				
VAT payable (refund)				
Drawings				
Total payments (b)				
Net cash flow (a-b)				
Opening bank balance				
Closing bank balance				

Business   Period Covered

Receipts	Month Budget Actual	Month Budget Actual	Month Budget Actual	Month Budget Actual
Cash Sales				
Cash from debtors				
Capital introduced				
Total receipts (a)				
Payments				
Payments to creditors				

Salaries/wages				
Rent/rates/water				
Insurance				
Repairs/renewals				
Heat/light/power				
Printing/stationary				
Motor and travel				
Telephone				
Professional fees				
Capital payments				
Interest and charges				
Other				
VAT payable (refund)				
Drawings				
Total payments (b)				
Net cash flow (a-b)				
Opening bank balance				
Closing bank balance				

The forecasting of other income

These entries will very much depend on the nature and type of your business. If you are VAT registered, and are fortunate enough to receive a refund then this will be a one off entry. There are a number of other items which may fit into this section, such as any loans given to the company by the owner, rent received from investments or finance from other sources.

Forecasting expenditure

The expenditure columns of the cash flow forecast are similarly divided into different sections. There are the cash purchases for those items where no credit is allowed, or no credit taken. There are creditors. This sum will represent those purchases where credit has been given. This sum will still have to be paid. This represents free finance and should be entered at the appropriate period when it is paid.

Salaries and wages and employers contributions

These expenses can be accurately predicted. The amount of PAYE will depend on the level of salaries and wages and will include National Insurance and income tax. There may be other contributions depending on the nature of your business and the overall deal offered. Pensions may represent one such payment.

The timing of your PAYE payment is of relevance to your tax return. If the monthly value due to HMRC is less than a certain figure, then it can be paid quarterly. If you exceed this amount then the payments must be made monthly. In both cases, the payments must be made on a certain date details of which can be obtained from HMRC.

Payments for use of energy

Payment for gas, electricity and any other energy sources will need to be included in this section. These payments will almost certainly be paid on a quarterly basis. Some companies, in particular those offering cheaper deals will sometimes insist on a monthly payment. This should be avoided if possible. There will be seasonal variations here, with winter costing more than summer and so on. These trends will have been recorded in your budget.

Payments for rent/service charge

Rental payments and other associated payments such as service charge and insurance payments for the building will normally be paid on a quarterly basis. It is highly unusual to pay these any more frequently. Rates due to the local authority will usually be made twice per year. However, this will depend on the local authority area and also your own agreement with them. It could be that you pay by monthly direct debit.

Bank and interest charges on overdrafts, loans and hire purchase

Bank charges will depend very much on how you manage your business and run your accounts. The more transactions the more the charges. You should be aware of the structure of charges, which relates to your particular bank and then you should analyse how you intend to run your business. If you handle a lot of cash, for example, particularly coins, it is likely to prove quite expensive to convert notes into coins. Alternative arrangements should be made, if possible. Bank charges do add up and it is necessary to enter these on the expenditure section of the cash flow forecast. Interest on overdrafts and repayments on loans and hire purchase should be entered if appropriate, in the loan repayments section. These can be interest payments on fixed loans or monthly charges payable on an ongoing overdraft.

Value Added Tax

The precise date of payment of VAT will vary. It is normally due every quarter but which quarter will depend on the date of registration of your business.

VAT applies to most sales and purchases within a business, if you are registered for VAT. However, building VAT into a cash flow forecast will be influenced on whether you are a cash business or account on an invoice basis. The timing on repayment or reimbursement of VAT is influenced by this factor.

When a budget is prepared, VAT is not included as a separate item. It is only necessary to look at the total price of sales. However, in relation to a cash flow forecast, the amount of VAT received and paid out has to be recorded separately. These are known respectively as the input (VAT paid out) and output (VAT received). HMRC are very vigilant indeed about collection of moneys due and also the way they are accounted for and it is absolutely necessary to keep clear records.

If you account for VAT on an invoice basis then it is the time that the goods are invoiced, and not the time that money is received, that must be considered.

Output tax on sales
As we have seen, VAT is accounted for by quarterly return and will be payable to the Customs and Excise at the end of the month following your VAT quarter. Therefore, if your VAT cycle is

from April to March 31st, then your return will be due 31st July-October-January-April 31st.

Accounting for VAT on a cash accounting basis

If you are using a cash accounting basis, then it is the time of payment that counts in relation to the VAT return. Therefore, you may sell goods and not receive payment for several months but it is the actual time of receipt of payment that counts for the VAT return.

Now read the key points from Chapter 5 overleaf.

****

Summary of Main Points From Chapter 5.

- A cash flow forecast deals with transactions at the time of payment. Sale of goods and final payment are not usually connected.

- Quite simply, a cash flow forecast will measure the supply and movement of cash. A bank, or any potential funder, will insist on seeing a well-prepared forecast.

- As with a budget, a cash flow forecast will run from month to month and include all elements of cash flow in the forecast.

****

6.
HOW TO MONITOR BUDGETS AND CASHFLOW

Chapter 6

Monitoring Budgets and Cashflow

Building on from the previous chapters, it can be seen that effective monitoring of budgets and cash flow entails regular scrutiny, the making of comparisons between what you have forecast and what is actually happening within your company.

On both the budget and cash flow there is a column entitled budget and actual. At the end of each given month it will be necessary to fill the actual column and measure this against expenditure and make appropriate revisions.

If things are seriously wrong then detailed analysis of your business activities is needed.

In many cases, there are crucial timing differences between income and expenditure which can cause problems. A typical budget and cash flow forecast, if all is going well will look like the example overleaf.

This is based on a publishing business, which has one month's credit with its suppliers and also gives one-month credit to its distributor. The unit cost is £7.99.

Sales

Budget	Jan	Feb	March	April	May
	2000	1500	3000	1750	2000
Sales Value	15980	11985	23970	13982.50	15980
Purchases	7500	5625	11250	6562.50	7500
Overheads	1440	1080	2160	1260	1440
Profit	7040	5280	10560	6160	7040

The planned cash flow forecast should therefore correspond to the one below.

Cashflow	Jan	Feb	Mar	Apr	May
Income					
Sales	15980	11985	23970	13982.50	15980
Expenditure					
Purchases	7500	5625	11250	6562.50	7500
Overheads	1440	1080	2160	1260	1440
Surplus/Deficit	7040	5280	4200	11460	5980
Opening balance	7040	5280	10560	6160	7040
Closing					

If, however, your customer is one month late when paying a bill, this will throw your cash flow out and you will have to revise the columns accordingly.

Those people who owe you money are called your debtors. Quite simply, they are in debt to you. It is vitally important that you maintain a system to monitor those who are in debt to you. Failure to do this will mean that you will be short of cash and your plan, based on your budget and your cash flow forecast, will not be accurate. It is best, when managing business, to have two sets of records for invoices, one for paid invoices and one for unpaid invoices.

Those debtors who are late with payment are called "aged debtors" and the records kept by you are called the aged debtors records. The analysis you carry out is called the aged debtor's analysis.

It is essential that you have a standard period within which you will send letters to debtors and a cut off period when you will take court action. Even if you pursue the customer for payment in the county court it is never sure that you will recover the debt. However, it is a matter of principle because cash flow management, as we have seen, is integral to your business.

Monitoring budgets

In addition to having to make adjustments to cash flow forecasts because of late payments and other reasons, it may be that you have overestimated your budget figures. In other words, you got the budget wrong. It is obviously very important to check the budget performance each month, i.e. budget against actual to make sure that performance in this area corresponds to your cash flow forecast. Larger businesses will prepare a full set of operating accounts each month in order to ensure that they have an ongoing accurate picture. For small business, this is obviously impractical and therefore an ongoing monitoring of the budget and cash flow forecasts is crucially important.

One area which can potentially cause you problems is that of stock. The value of stock will often not vary from month to month though there may be seasonal trends. If the stock does vary a lot, and is giving cause for concern you have two alternative courses of action:

- Take stock each month and evaluate its costs

- Introduce a stock control system. This is the favoured approach as it is less time consuming. You record the amount of each line of stock on a separate account so that you can quickly evaluate its value.

Excessive stocks tie up much needed cash and will be a drain on your company's liquidity. There are a number of ways of deducing the amount of stock that you should carry.

The important factors are:
- The amount of sales of that particular product
- Delivery times
- Discount policies on purchase
- The size of raw material batches ordered
- The value of the stock

You should be able to deduce an accurate stock level by looking at previous sales and the amount of stock consumed and projecting this forward to correspond to future sales. You will need a careful analysis of needs because obviously bulk buying at a discount will play a part. However, even if bulk buying, much needed capital could needlessly be tied up. The longer term cash benefits of discount must be weighed against ongoing sales and profit.

The use of financial ratios for monitoring budgets and cash flow

A financial ratio entails deducing the correlation between two figures and ascertaining the meaning of that correlation. There are four types of financial ratios:

- Profit ratios-these show how efficient the business is, or how good it is, at making profit from capital invested.

- Efficiency ratios-these show the management efficiency of the business.

- Liquidity ratios-these ratios measure the working capital within the business

- Solvency ratios-they show how solvent the business is or how near it is to going bankrupt.

Profit ratios

There are three useful ratios, which indicate how profitable your business is:

- The gross profit margin

- The net profit margin

- The return on capital employed within your business

The gross profit margin is probably the most important ratio. The gross profit calculates the relationship between the gross profit and sales by the following method:

$$\frac{\text{Gross profit times 1000}}{\text{Sales}}$$

= Gross profit margin

The net profit margin shows you the ratio after the deduction of all expenses of the business except tax. It is not as reliable an indicator as the gross profit margin but can be useful. It is calculated as follows:

$$\frac{\text{Net profit times 100}}{\text{Sales}}$$

= Net profit margin

The return on capital ratio measures the revenue being generated from the capital employed in the business. This ratio enables you to compare the income produced by the business with income from other forms of investment. The ratio is calculated as follows:

$$\frac{\text{Profit before charging interest and tax}}{\text{Total capital employed}}$$

= Total capital employed

Efficiency ratios

Efficiency ratios divide into three areas each of which are further subdivided:

- Debtors

Debtor's turnover ratio

Debtor's collection period

- Creditors

Creditors turnover ratio

Creditors payment period

- Stock

Stock turnover ratio

Average stock holding period

These particular measurements show just how efficiently the capital utilised by the business is being used. The debtor turnover ratio shows the number of times that the unpaid debt is "turned over". It is calculated like so:

Sales (+ VAT)

   Debtors

= Debtors turnover ratio

The debtor's collection period is a more useful ratio for measurement. This shows the average number of days that it takes you to collect your debts:

Debtors times 365

Sales + (VAT)

= Debtor collection period (in days)

You can check the creditors turnover ratio in a similar way and also the creditors payment period:

Purchases (+VAT)

Creditors

= Creditors turnover ratio

Creditors times 365

Purchases (+VAT)

= Creditor payment period

It is important to monitor the creditor period as well as the debtor's periods as you can run into trouble if you yourself become a debtor and run the risk of losing credit.

The final ratios here are the stock ratios. In the same manner as the ratios for debtors and creditors are measured, the stock turnover ratio and the average stock holding period can be calculated in the following way:

$$\frac{\text{Cost of sales}}{\text{Stock at cost}}$$

= Stock turnover ratio

and

$$\frac{\text{Stock at cost times 365}}{\text{Cost of sales}}$$

= Average stock holding period

Liquidity ratios

Important ratios for any business are those measuring liquidity. The following will be outlined:

- The current ratio
- The quick ratio
- The security interval

The liquidity ratios show the ability of the business to meet its liabilities as they fall due from its assets. A business should have sufficient current assets to cover its current liabilities. The current ratio measures the ability of a business to achieve this, in this way:

Current assets

Current liabilities

= Current ratio

As discussed, current assets are items such as stock, work in progress, cash in the bank, debtors and cash at hand. Current liabilities are amounts owed by the business to its creditors and bank overdrafts. Current liabilities do not include items such as long term loans, which do not normally fall due for repayment within 12 months.

The current ratio will usually be between 1.5 and 2. If it is less than 1, you are probably relying on a bank overdraft secured on the long term assets of the business, or delaying payments to your creditors. Whatever the situation, the requirement for working capital should be of some concern.

If this ratio exceeds 2 then you may not be making the best use of your current assets. You may have too much cash in the bank or too much stock or to many debtors.

Checking the quick ratio

The current ratio checks all current assets and current liabilities. A better way, or test, is to check on those assets, which are cash, or near cash. This is the relevance of the quick ratio.

Assets such as stock and work in progress may be difficult to sell and covert into cash to pay the liabilities of the business and so these are excluded.

Only those quick assets that are left-cash, money at the bank and debtors, are included. The ratio is calculated as follows:

Quick assets
_____
Current liabilities

= Quick ratio

This ratio is usually between 0.7 and 1, although the nature of a particular business will affect this.

The security interval

This particular ratio measures how long the business could survive if no more cash was received but if it continued to pay its normal expenses. It is calculated as follows:

Quick assets

Operating expenses (expressed as daily figure)

= Security interval

This interval is usually between 30 and 90 days, although depends on the type of business.

Solvency ratios

There are two ratios in this group:
- The solvency ratio
- Gearing

If your total liabilities exceed your total assets then your business is technically insolvent. This is expressed as the solvency ratio, expressed as follows:

Total assets of the business

Total liabilities of the business

= Solvency ratio

If this equation produces a ratio of less than 1 then you are insolvent. This is an are that you must keep under careful review, as you may reach a point when you cannot trade due to the inability to meet liabilities. Even if the ratio is greater than 1, you cannot always feel totally secure. This is why the corresponding use of liquidity ratios is so important.

Checking gearing

The ratio of money that a business has loaned to the capital invested in the business by shareholders or the owners of the business is referred to as the gearing of the business. This includes accumulated profits if they have not been withdrawn. It is calculated as follows:

Total borrowed

Owners capital

= Gearing

The gearing of a business is an important guide to how much the business should be allowed to borrow. In general, banks expect their lending to the business to be at least matched by the investment of the owners and shareholders. This means that a ratio of less than 1 should be expected.

By using ratios you can check on trends and financial health of your business and also make a comparison with similar business as your own.

Now read the key points from chapter 6

****

Summary of Main Points From Chapter 6.

- Effective monitoring of budgets and cash flow entails regular scrutiny, making comparisons between what you have forecast and what is actually happening with your company.

- The effective control of credit given to your customers is of the utmost importance. It is essential that you have a credit control system in place which consists of standard letters and, in the final analysis, court action against persistent debtors.

- One area of a business that can cause particular problems is that of stock regulation. It is essential that any business with stockholding has in place a stock control system. Excess stock ties up capital needlessly and can have a longer term detrimental effect.

****

7.

BASIC TIPS FOR USING TECHNOLOGY-SPREADSHEETS AS A TOOL

Chapter 7

Using Technology-Basic Advice for Non-Technical People.

For a long time, the preferred method, through necessity, for the preparation of budgets and accounts for business was by maintaining ledgers by hand. This method has changed rapidly over the years, through the introduction of accounts packages, such as Quickbooks and many more, in new technology. Within all packages, the spreadsheet has become an indispensable tool for many businesses, both large and small.

Most computers are now run through windows. The main spreadsheet programmes running under windows is Excel. Although there are different operating systems, we will concentrate on Excel in this chapter.

Using a spreadsheet

All spreadsheets are essentially the same. The origins of spreadsheets date from the accountants paper with its lines and columns. The main difference between spreadsheets and manually kept calculations is that a spreadsheet is maintained on a computer and the data is input by hand, with changes to all aspects of the spreadsheet automatically happening when a figure is changed.

For example, if a row of numbers adds up to a specific figure then a change to any one of those numbers will also change the bottom line.

The actual sheet on the computer screen is not simply one sheet of A$. It is a large sheet, consisting of columns and rows. Usually there will be up to 256 columns and 8192 rows. The computer screen is a window which enables the user to focus in on a specific area of the spreadsheet.

Across the top of the worksheet are letters to identify the columns. These are A,B,C...X,Y,Z, AA, AB, AC...AX,AY,AZ, and so on.

Down the side of the sheet are the row numbers. In this way the sheet is divided into a maximum of 2,097,152 cells, each of which can be addressed by specifying the column and row number.

Each cell on the spreadsheet can contain either data or a formula. The formula is quite often an instruction to add up or subtract and is linked by Cell links from cell to cell.

A sample spreadsheet is shown overleaf.

Advantages of spreadsheets

There are many advantages of using a spreadsheet:

- Spreadsheets are easy to use

- Spreadsheets remove the need for endless calculations and also removes the human error factor

- Budgets and forecasts are easy to modify on a spreadsheet

Disadvantages of using a spreadsheet

- You need to acquire a working knowledge of a spreadsheet so that you can utilise it effectively. Not everyone is computer literate and may find that they can more easily keep records manually

Sample Spreadsheet

	A	B	C	D	E	F	G
1							
2							
3							
4				**Cell D3**			
5							
6							
7							
8							
9				**Cell D9**			
10							
11				**Sum (D3.D9)**			
12							
13							

As you can see, the advantages far outweigh the disadvantages and it is rapidly becoming the nor for those who keep their own accounts to use a spreadsheet.

There are numerous courses available, low cost courses which can introduce people to spreadsheets and provide adequate basic training. The costs of packages now are low and any newly acquired computer will almost certainly contain a package, most often Excel, which comes with nearly all Microsoft windows applications.

****

Useful addresses and websites

Association of Taxation Technicians

30 Monck Street

London

SW1P 2AP

Phone: +44 (0)20 7340 0551

e-mail: info@att.org.uk

www.att.org.uk

Association of Certified Chartered Accounts (ACCA)

www.accaglobal.com

Institute of Chartered Accountants England and Wales

ICAEW

Chartered Accountants' Hall

1 Moorgate Place,

London

EC2R 6EA

www.icaew.com

020 7920 8100

Institute Members Scotland

PO Box 26198

Dumfermline, KY12 8ZD - 0131 1251

Chartered Accountants Ireland

Chartered Accountants House,

47-49 Pearse Street,

Dublin 2

Chartered Accountants House,

32-38 Linenhall Street,

Belfast,

County Antrim

BT2 8BG,

United Kingdom

www. charteredaccountants.i.e

Chartered Institute of Taxation

30 Monck Street
London SW1P 2AP

Phone: +44 (0)20 7340 0550

www.tax.org.uk

The Association of Accounting Technicians.

140 Aldersgate Street,

London

 EC1A 4HY

www.aat.org.uk

The Financial Conduct Authority

12 Endeavour Square

London E20 1JN

0800 111 6768

https://www.fca.org.uk/

Government Departments

HMRC

www.gov.uk/government/organisations/hm-revenue-customs

The Insolvency Service

www.gov.uk/government/organisations/insolvency-service

Department for Work and Pensions

www.gov.uk/government/organisations/department-for-work-
pensions

Pensions-The Pensions Regulator

www.thepensionsregulator.gov.uk

Auto-Enrolment

www.autoenrolment.co.uk

Department for Business Innovation and Skills

www.gov.uk/government/organisations/department-for-business-innovation-skills

****

Glossary of terms

Accounting ratios

A set of ratios used to indicate a particular financial position of a company.

Aged debtors

This term is used to highlight those people who have been in debt for a longer period than the norm. It is normal practice to age debts in terms of months so that when a debt becomes a problem it requires chasing and settling.

Balance sheet

A statement of the worth of the business at the accounting date expressed in terms of historical cost.

Break even point

The point at which production equals the fixed cost-the point at which you break even.

Budgets

A financial/quantitative statement, prepared prior to an accounting period which forecasts future expenditure. The budget is used as a planning tool and is essential for the effective management of business.

Capital expenditure

Expenditure on fixed assets which have a lasting benefit to the business.

Cash flow forecast

A forecast showing the budgeted receipts and payments for the forthcoming year (or period).

Credit period

The period between the supply and invoicing of goods and services and the payment of the invoice.

Creditors

The suppliers to the business to whom money is owed and the amount owed by the business to them.

Current assets

These are assets which are either cash or can be turned into cash quite quickly. They include cash, bank balances, debtors. Stock and work in progress.

Current liabilities

These are amounts owed to suppliers (creditors) together with short term loans such as bank overdrafts,

Debtors

Those who owe money to the business

Depreciation

An allowance made for the reduction or dimunition of the value of fixed
assets.

Direct costs

Direct costs are those costs directly related to the production of the product.

Fixed assets

Property and equipment owned by a business which will have a long lasting benefit to the business.

Fixed costs

A fixed cost is a cost which is unaffected by variations in a firms production. A fixed cost may be rent, rates etc.

Gross profit

The profit earned by a business from trading, prior to the deduction of overhead expenses.

Indirect costs

Indirect costs are those costs which do not relate directly to the production of the product but are necessary to provide the setting within which the business is run.

Key ratios

Key ratios measure the performance of a business in a way that conventional analysis cannot. These ratios are essential to provide a picture of where the business is.

Long term liabilities

Amounts owed by a business which are not due for payment within one year.

Net assets

Net assets are the total assets of the business minus its liabilities.

Net profit

The profit of a business after taking account of all its expenses.

Overheads

Money spent regularly to keep the business running. Overheads include rent, rates, salaries etc.

Profit and loss account

An account summarising the income and expenditure of a business for a given period and showing the surplus and deficit.

Quick assets

This is a subdivision of current assets, comprising assets which can realise cash quickly if needed.

Revenue expenditure

Revenue expenditure is wholly used up during the accounting period. Examples of revenue expenditure include raw materials, payment of rent and salaries.

****

Index

Accountancy and audit fees, 6, 77
Advantages of spreadsheets, 8, 121
Analysed Cash book System, 4, 34

Bank charges, 6, 56, 73, 76, 94
Break even analysis, 6, 71
Budgeting for capital items, 6, 78
Budgeting for overheads, 6, 73
Budgeting sales income, 6, 65
Budgets, 1, 3, 5, 53, 54, 61, 121, 129

Calculating the break even point, 6, 71
Capital expenditure, 78, 130
Cash flow, 5, 52, 54, 85, 130
Computerised Accounting Systems, 5, 43
Cost of sales, 81, 110
Costs involved in business, 5, 63
Costs of production, 6, 68, 69
Creditors, 108, 109, 130
Current assets, 111, 130
Current liabilities, 111, 112, 131

Debtors, 7, 87, 108, 109, 131
Depreciation, 6, 56, 73, 77, 80, 131

Disadvantages of using a spreadsheet, 8, 121
Double Entry System, 5, 43
Efficiency ratios, 106, 108
Entertaining, 6, 73, 77, 80

Fixed and variable costs, 5, 63
Fixed assets, 131
Forecasting cash flow, 7, 87
Forecasting expenditure, 7, 92

Gearing, 113, 114
Gross profit, 56, 107, 132

HM Revenue and Customs, 32
HMRC, 34

Income and Expenditure Account, 32
Insurance, 6, 56, 73, 74, 76, 80, 89, 91, 92

Key ratios, 132

Liquidity ratios, 8, 106, 110

Management Accounting, 5, 51
Monitoring of budgets, 101

National Insurance Contributions, 74

Net assets, 132
Net profit margin, 107
Overheads-sales budgets, 62

PAYE, 92, 93
Pension contributions, 74
Pensions, 127, 128
Petty cash, 31
Profit and loss account, 133
Profit ratios, 8, 106
Proprietary systems, 4, 33
Purchase invoices, 31

Rent and rates, 6, 73, 74, 80
Revenue, 32
Revenue expenditure, 133

Salaries, 6, 7, 73, 74, 80, 89, 91, 92
Sales budget-cost of sales, 62
Sales budget-production budget, 61
Selling expenses, 6, 64
Semi-variable costs, 5, 64
Solvency ratios, 8, 106, 113
Stationary, 6, 73, 74, 80

The cash flow forecast, 7, 85
Travelling, 6, 73, 75, 80

Using a spreadsheet, 8, 119Value Added Tax, 7, 94

VAT, 30, 31, 32, 35

Wages, 31

****

Emerald Guides

www.straightforwardco.co.uk

Titles in the Emerald Series:

Law

Guide to Bankruptcy

Conducting Your Own Court case

Guide to Consumer law

Creating a Will

Guide to Family Law

Guide to Employment Law

Guide to European Union Law

Guide to Health and Safety Law

Guide to Criminal Law

Guide to Landlord and Tenant Law

Guide to the English Legal System

Guide to Housing Law

Guide to Marriage and Divorce

Guide to The Civil Partnerships Act

Guide to The Law of Contract

The Path to Justice

You and Your Legal Rights

Powers of Attorney

Managing Divorce and Separation

Health

Guide to Combating Child Obesity

Asthma Begins at Home

Alternative Health and Alternative Remedies

Explaining Arthritis

Music

How to Survive and Succeed in the Music Industry

General

A Practical Guide to Obtaining probate

A Practical Guide to Residential Conveyancing

Writing The Perfect CV

Keeping Books and Accounts-A Small Business Guide

Business Start Up-A Guide for New Business

Finding Asperger Syndrome in the Family-A Book of Answers

Explaining Autism Spectrum Disorder

Explaining Alzheimers

Explaining Parkinsons

Writing True Crime

Becoming a Professional Writer

Writing your Autobiography

For details of the above titles published in the Emerald Guides Series go to:

www.straightforwardco.co.uk

Companion books in the Emerald Business Series

Business Start up and Future Planning £9.99

Keeping Books and Accounts £9.99

Emerald Guides

© Straightforward Co Ltd 2019

British Library Cataloguing in Publication Data. A catalogue record is available for this book from the British library.

ISBN: 978-1-84716-945-7

Printed by 4edge www.4edge.co.uk
Cover design by BW-Studio Derby

Emerald Business Management

Setting Budgets And Managing Cash flows

Jennifer Rhodes

Editor: Roger Sproston